MAKE ME A
PRINCESS

Ticktock

MAKE ME A
PRINCESS

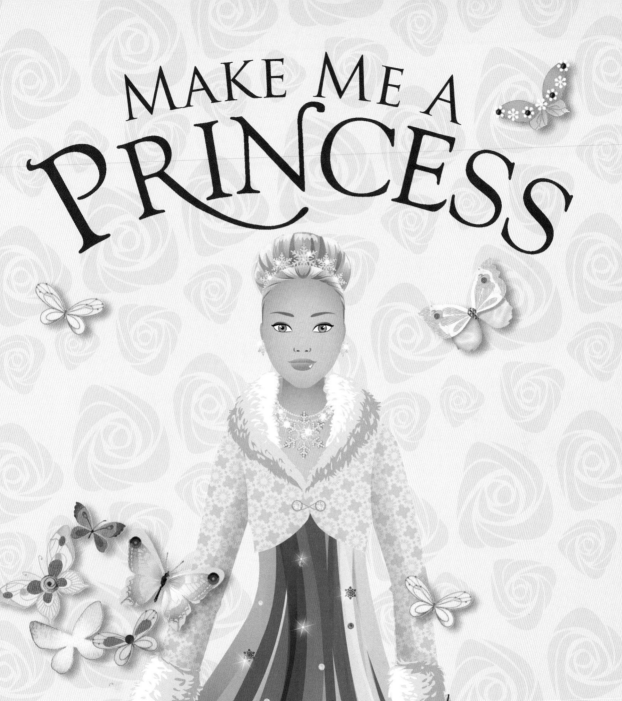

Contents

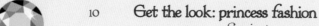

6   What makes a princess?

8   Your princess profile

10   **Get the look: princess fashion**
    12   Spring
    14   Summer
    16   Fall
    18   Winter
    20   Shoes
    22   Bags

24   **Beauty secrets: princess pampering**
    26   Magic facial massage
    28   Sparkling eyes
    30   Nails... naturally
    32   Princess polish
    34   Dazzling designs
    36   Perfect princess pedicure

38   **Crowning glory: taming your lovely locks**
    40   Treat your tresses
    42   Princess spring style
    42   Simple summer style
    46   Fall waves
    48   Winter glamor
    50   The ultimate up-do
    52   Perfect princess twists
    54   Sixty-second styles

56   **Sparkling jewels and twinkling tiaras**
    58   Which jewel is right for you?
    60   Design your own tiara
    62   Dazzling rings
    64   Pretty button bracelet
    66   Princess pendants

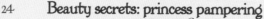

Contents

68   Princess friendship bracelets
70   Make a princess petal brooch

Plush palaces: homes fit for a princess   72
74   Your dream palace
76   Pretty princess bedroom
78   Treasure box
80   Perfect photo frame
82   Bedroom bunting

On your best behavior: perfect princess poise   84
86   Princess Ps and Qs
88   Banqueting behavior
90   Being kind to others
92   Curtsy like a princess

Parties, princess-style   94
96   Invitations
98   Preparty pamper
100   Princess party
102   Party games
104   Super sleepovers
106   Sleepover style
108   Travelling in style
110   Design your perfect carriage

The perfect prince   112
114   Prince predictor
116   Your dream princess wedding
118   How to dance like Cinderella
120   Rate your princess progress
122   Your top-to-toe princess checklist

124   Princess words

126   Index

What makes a princess?

There's more to being a princess than wearing a sparkly tiara and a pretty dress. Being kind to others and having perfect manners are just as important as looking superstylish!

Everything you need to achieve princess perfection is in this book – from beauty basics to throwing the party of the century. So make yourself comfortable and read on. Your princess journey has begun!

a princess sparkles, whatever the occasion!

Your top-to-toe
transformation
starts here....

Your princess profile

Quiet and thoughtful or party girl, what type of princess are you?

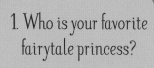

1. Who is your favorite fairytale princess?

a. Sleeping Beauty
b. Snow White
c. Cinderella

2. What would you wear to a royal ball?

a. A white silk gown and glass slippers
b. A floral frock and golden sandals
c. A red velvet dress and ruby shoes

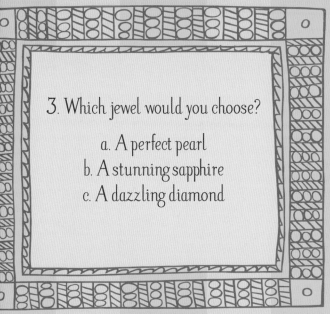

3. Which jewel would you choose?

    a. A perfect pearl
    b. A stunning sapphire
    c. A dazzling diamond

4. What would you call
a beautiful white pony?

    a. Magic Moonlight
    b. White Lightning
    c. Snow Dancer

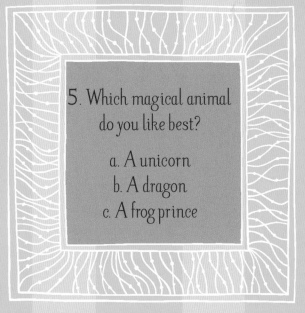

5. Which magical animal
do you like best?

    a. A unicorn
    b. A dragon
    c. A frog prince

Your profile

Count your a, b, and c answers. Mostly a: Thoughtful and dreamy, you understand others and are a true friend. Mostly b: Loyal and brave, you love nature and care about our world. Mostly c: You're a party princess, who loves to meet and mingle. A mixture of a, b, and c: Sensitive, lively, and fun – *you really are a perfect princess!*

Get the look: princess fashion

For a true princess, fabulous fabrics and shimmering jewels are always in fashion, but each season also brings its own ideas and inspiration to keep her looking lovely all year long.

Read on for tips to set your own seasonal style.

Spring

Key colors for your spring wardrobe include daffodil yellow and pastel brights inspired by spring flowers. Think bluebell, primrose, and cherry-blossom pink.

Buttoned-up, fitted winter styles are replaced by fluid fabric and a few frills and flounces.

Choose jewelry to complement your spring look. A gold tiara with glittering amethysts is perfect for petal pinks and soft purples. Or, choose a sparkling silver tiara with multicolored gems in this season's pretty pastels. Whatever the outfit, springtime sparkle is a must!

Why not have fun with fashion motifs to suit your personality? Choose flowers, butterflies, stars, hearts, or your own special theme to personalize your style.

Summer

For a princess who wants to look hot as well as cool, summer is a time for floaty fabrics in cute, candy colors.

Pinks and purples are girly but glam. Shimmering fabrics dazzle in bright sunlight, while jewelry can be bold, with large statement pieces.

note this *fan*-tastic way to keep cool!

To stay cool when it's hot, wear your hair off your face. Keep it tied back with sequinned bands or flowing scarves for film-star chic.

sheer fabric is perfect for a light, fresh feel

Gold, jewelled sandals keep feet cool with strappy, snappy style. Glamorous sunglasses complete a sizzling summer look.

Fall

When woodlands dazzle in shades of orange, yellow, red, and brown, so does a season-savvy princess. These colors work together in any combination, while gold jewelry and accessories add to the mellow richness of autumnal shades.

leaf-shaped motifs work beautiful

Layers are the answer to the season's changeable weather. A light wrap or shawl, thrown over your dress, gives warmth and swirly style.

Glittering golds combined with all shades of orange will give any girl an autumnal glow. Alternatively, try rich jewel colors instead. Sapphire blue or emerald green are perfect!

gold jewelry adds glamor to any fall outfit

If you're a redhead, this is your season, but for everyone, shiny, tumbling locks are the way to go.

Winter

A princess is cool but she's never cold, because she dresses for the season and looks incredible – even in the most wintry weather.

Icy pinks and blues, shimmering silver, and snowy white fill her wardrobe. Warm fabrics are superimportant – wool and velvet give a luxurious look but are comfortable and cosy.

A swirling cloak trimmed with fun fake fur works over any princess dress, and a hood protects her shiny hair and twinkling tiara.

silver, platinum, and diamonds add icy sparkle

ankle boots with fake fur trim are cute and cosy

pom-poms are pretty on princess pumps

Shoes

Just because your gown sweeps the floor, it doesn't mean you can forget about your feet! A flash of jewelled footwear looks divine, while sweet little satin ballet pumps suit almost any outfit.

dancing shoes help
princess toes to twinkle!

summer sandals studded
with jewels are perfect!

A princess knows that no girl can have too many shoes. That's why she always has the perfect pair for every royal occasion.

Bags

Every princess needs a few elegant
essentials when she's out and about — and
a beautiful bag to carry them. Choose one
to match your dress or use it to add a pop of
contrasting color to your look.

a sweet dolly bag with feather trim

Don't forget your bag can be as
decorative as your dress. Think jewels,
sequins, and silk flowers for evening
and tassels, fringes, and charms
for daytime.

a classic clutch patterned with crystals

a shoulder bag for hands-free ease

Now design your own bag. Start by thinking about all the things you need to carry. Tissues? Lip gloss? A brush? Money? A spare tiara? A phone?

Then find some paper and draw your dream bag. Have fun with shape, color, and delicious detail.

Beauty secrets: princess pampering

Every princess knows that pampering is essential to keep her in tip-top shape. Looking after herself by eating healthily and getting plenty of fresh air and exercise, as well as making sure she gets her beauty sleep, means she always looks great!

Follow these beauty tips to make sure you glow from top to toe!

Magic facial massage

This relaxing step-by-step routine will make sure your face always has real princess radiance.

1 Sitting comfortably, use your middle fingers to make gentle circles on your temples.

2 Place your fingertips on your forehead, and lightly and smoothly stroke to the sides.

3 With middle fingers, stroke along your eyebrows from above your nose to the ends.

4 Starting at your chin, very gently pinch along your jawline towards your ears.

5 With middle fingers, smooth down the sides of your nose in long strokes.

6 With your palms at jaw level, gently smooth upwards over your cheeks.

Sparkling eyes

Revive tired eyes and skin with this simple cucumber treatment.
You'll soon have your sparkle back!

1 Put the chopped cucumber and water in a jar. Put it in the fridge to cool.

2 Dip a cotton pad in the cucumber water and gently wipe it over your face.

3 Using a fresh pad, wipe carefully across your closed eyelids with the cool liquid.

4 Gently pat your face dry with a towel.

5 Lie down and relax with a cucumber slice on each of your closed eyes.

Wear sunglasses and protect your skin with sunscreen in summer.

Nails... naturally

Make sure your fingers are always princess pretty with this simple routine.

You will need:

* nail file
* bowl of warm water
* towel
* hand cream

1 Gently file your nails into a pretty shape, smoothing off any rough edges.

2 Always file in one direction, not with a sawing motion, from the center to the sides.

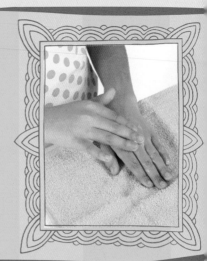

3 Soak your fingers in warm water for five minutes.

4 Dry your hands carefully and smooth hand cream generously over both hands.

5 Gently massage the back of each hand with the fingers of the other hand.

Princess polish

Here's how to apply polish perfectly for royal waving and greeting!

You will need:
* nail polish
* two hand towels
* nail polish remover
* cotton swabs

1 Make sure your nails are clean and dry. Place one hand flat on an old towel.

2 Paint a stripe down the center of each nail, with another stripe either side if necessary.

3 Wave your hands to your favorite pop song. Your nails will be dry by the end!

4 Use a little remover on a cotton swab to clean up if you make tiny mistakes.

Dazzling designs

Here are some fun ideas for party-perfect nails. Try them, then invent some of your own!

You will need:
* nail polishes
* nail gems and stickers

1 Paint your nails and, once they are dry, add nail stickers for instant glamor.

2 Or, while the polish is still tacky, gently add flowers or other nail art.

3 Once you have finished, add a final coat of clear polish to keep your funky designs looking beautiful!

Perfect princess pedicure

Here's how to make sure your feet look fabulous all summer long.

You will need:

- large bowl of warm water
- body or foot lotion
- towel
- nail clippers
- nail file
- nail polish (optional)

1 Soak your feet for five minutes in the warm water.

2 Dry your feet carefully, especially between your toes!

3 Trim toenails straight across with clippers and smooth with a file if necessary.

4 Massage lotion into your feet, avoiding your nails if you want to paint them.

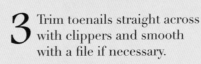

Apply polish in a pretty color.
Don't try to put on your shoes until it's really dry!

Crowning glory: taming your lovely locks

A princess knows her hair is her crowning glory.
To make sure her locks look luscious, she gives
them regular treatments and always looks
superstylish.

Follow these steps to tame your tresses and make
sure you look your best, whatever the occasion.

Treat your tresses

These fragrant herbal treatments will give your lovely locks natural princess beauty.

For fair hair
you will need:

❋ bowl
❋ towel
❋ 1 camomile
   tea bag
❋ mug of hot water

1 Put the tea bag and water in the bowl. Leave to cool while you wash your hair as usual.

2 Pour the water over your hair. Rinse, then wrap your hair in a towel to dry.

For red or dark hair
you will need:

❋ bowl
❋ 2–3 sprigs of
   rosemary
❋ mug of hot water
❋ towel

1 Put the rosemary and water in the bowl. Wash your hair as usual while the water cools.

2 Pour the water over your hair. Rinse, then wrap your hair in a towel to dry.

Princess spring style

This sweet and simple fishtail plait can be decorated for extra impact.

You will need:
- brush or comb
- styling spray
- a hair tie
- accessories to decorate

1 Gently brush your hair until it is smooth and tangle-free.

2 Spritz your hair all over with the styling spray.

3 Divide the top into two sections. Wrap a small piece from under the right section over and to the left.

4 Repeat with a piece from under the left side. Keep alternating sides, securing the end with a tie.

It's easier if you plait
a princess pal's hair
and she does yours!

Simple summer style

There is nothing like blow-drying for achieving a natural, swingy style, just right for summer.

You Will need:

* towel
* styling spray
* hair clips
* round brush
* blow-dryer
* hair spray

1 Shampoo and condition your hair as usual, then gently towel dry.

2 Spritz your slightly damp hair lightly all over with styling spray.

3 Starting at the back, take one section of hair and clip the rest out of the way.

4 Direct the blow-dryer onto the section and slowly brush through it until dry.

5 As you finish a section, spritz it with hair spray, until your summer style is complete!

Fall waves

Here's the perfect look for windswept fall – tumbling tantalizing waves to toss.

You will need:
* hair clips
* styling spray
* round brush
* blow-dryer
* hair spray

1 Brush clean, dry hair, then pin the hair on the top of your head out of the way.

2 Generously spritz the end on the lower layer with styling spray.

3 Take a small section, wrap the spritzed hair around the brush, and dry it thoroughly.

4 Move on, a section at a time, until all the hair, including the top layer, has been styled.

5 Use plenty of hair spray to ke your curls until you are ready to wash or brush them out.

Winter glamor

This stunning style is superfast but perfect for sparkling evening parties.

1 Pull your hair into a low ponytail. Secure it with a hair tie.

2 Divide the ponytail into three strands. Divide the strands into three again and make three pla

3 Curl one of the plaits around and pin it into place using bobby pins.

4 Twist the other plaits in the same way and secure into a bun with bobby pins.

Add sparkling clips or hair jewels for evening glamor.

The ultimate up-do

Here's a sophisticated style that makes you the belle of any ball with real princess pizzazz.

You will need:
- brush or comb
- hair tie
- bobby pins and hair clips
- hair donut
- hair spray

1 Brush your hair up to make a ponytail on the very top of your head.

2 Pull your ponytail gently through the center of the donut.

3 Wrap your hair over and around the donut.

4 Tuck in the ends and secure everything with bobby pins so that the bun is firm.

5 Add flowers to decorate and use hair spray to smooth down any short, flyaway hairs.

Perfect princess twists

With a princess pal to help you, this sweet style is simplicity itself.

You will need:

* brush or comb
* 2 hair ties
* bobby pins
* flower clip
* a friend to help!!

1 Ask your friend to take a front section of your hair and divide it into two.

2 Twist the right half over and over the left all the way to the bottom.

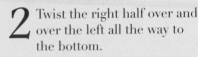

3 Pin up the first twist and make a second twist on the same side, as shown.

4 Repeat steps 2 and 3 on the other side.

5 Once you have finished the twists, hold them in place using hair ties.

This style's pretty when decorated with a lovely flower clip!

Sixty-second styles

Every princess needs some quick fixes when she wants to be ready in a magic minute.

To change her style in seconds, a true princess always has in her bag:

* hairbrush or comb
* headscarf
* hair tie
* flower clip
* spare tiara!

1 Brush your hair over to one side and make a low ponytail. Simple and sweet.

2 Use a pretty scarf as a headband for an instant Hollywood hairdo.

3 Add instant drama with a larger-than-life flower clip.

4 A single high ponytail is slick and sophisticated.

5 Pull your hair into a low ponytail, plait it, and add flowers for a fresh look.

If in doubt, a tiara adds a touch of class to any hairstyle!

Sparkling jewels and twinkling tiaras

Princesses always sparkle, but they can't resist adding gorgeous gems and jewels to their outfit for truly glittering glamor.

Choosing the right jewelry is as vital as selecting a stunning gown. Read on to find out how to pick the right accessories to make sure you shimmer and shine, whatever the occasion!

Which jewel is right for you?

January: a deep red *garnet*

Enjoy choosing gems to match your eyes, your dress, or your mood – or choose your princess birthstone for a special signature sparkle.

February: a delicate purple *amethyst*

March: a shimmering green-blue *aquamarine*

April: a glittering *diamond*

May: a gorgeous green *emerald*

June: a pure white *pearl*

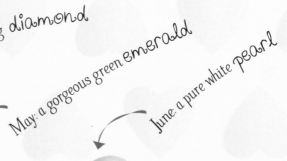

July: a rich red ruby

August: a glowing green peridot

September: a brilliant blue sapphire

October: an amazing multicolored opal

November: an awesome orange topaz

Genuine jewels make you feel like a million dollars – and may cost as much! Fakes are just as fabulous, and much lighter on the bank balance!

December: an ocean-blue turquoise

Design your own tiara

A true princess doesn't set foot outside the palace without her tiara... made from the finest gold or silver and studded with a host of glittering jewels. What kind of tiara would you choose to crown your perfect princess look?

Use these tempting tiaras as inspiration, then draw your own perfect headpiece.

tick on sequins for extra *sparkle!*

stick-on *gems* will give your tiara a really royal finish!

add *glitter* for that extra bit of *bling*

Dazzling rings

You will need:
- pipe cleaner
- pencil
- glitter glue or stick-on jewels

Make fabulous flower rings for every finger with this easy princess project.

1 Starting 2 inches (5 cm) from the end of the pipe cleaner, wrap it around the pencil, then twist it once to make a loop.

2 Keep making loops next to each other until you have six in a row.

3 Bend the loops around into a circle and twist the ends once to secure.

4 Twist the ends together into a ring shape to fit your finger. Add glitter glue or stick-on jewels to decorate.

Make a range of
rings to add glitz to
any gown.

Pretty button bracelet

You will need:

* thin elastic
* scissors*
* buttons
* glitter glue or stick-on jewels

An asterisk (*) means always ask an adult to help you with this step.

1 Cut a piece of elastic long enough to wrap around your wrist twice.*

2 Choose buttons for your bracelet. Thread the elastic through two holes on each button so they lie flat.

3 Knot the ends of the elastic to fit your wrist. Add glitter glue or stick-on jewels for gorgeous glamor.

Choose dazzling colors to complement your clothes.

Princess pendants

Express your princess personality by designing your very own
pendant in scintillating silver.

You will need:
* cardboard
* scissors*
* string
* aluminum foil
* school glue
* jewels or glitter glue
* ribbon or cord

An asterisk (*) means
always ask an adult to
help you with this step.

1 Cut a shape from cardboard.
Pierce a hole in the top edge.
Brush glue over one side.*

2 Use string to make a pretty
pattern like the one above –
or design your own.

3 Leave to dry. Then
brush on more glue
and lay foil on top.

4 Press the foil down very
gently with your fingers.

5 Use jewels or glitter glue to
decorate your pendant, then
thread it on to the ribbon.

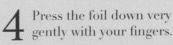

Princess friendship bracelets

1 Take three colored ribbons, cords, or strands of wool about 15 inches (40 cm) long.

2 Knot the strands 2 inches (4 cm) from one end. Put a heavy book on the knot. Spread out the strands.

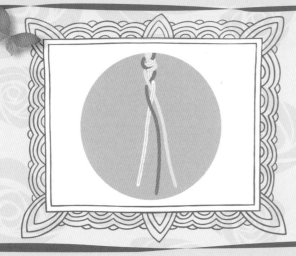

3 Put the strand on the left over the middle one. Then put the one on the right over the middle one.

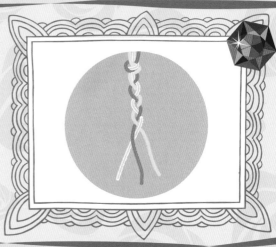

4 Keep going (left, right, left, right) to the end. Knot the end, then give your bracelet to a friend!

Tie the bracelet to your
princess pal's wrist and hope
she's made one for you, too!
An armful of bracelets shows
you're a popular princess!

Make a princess petal brooch

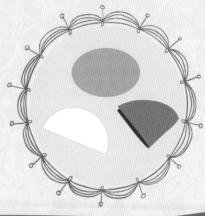

1 Using the cup or glass, draw five circles on the fabric and cut them out.*

2 Fold each circle in half, then half again, with the right side outside.

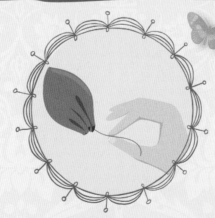

3 Take one piece and stitch around the curved edge.*

4 Gently pull the thread to gather the fabric into a petal shape.*

5 Without cutting the thread, do the same with the other petals.*

6 Stitch the last petal to the first to make a flower shape.*

7 Use school glue to fix a jewel or pretty button to the flower center.

add ribbon to make a pretty bracelet

Sew a safety pin or hair clip to the back to flaunt your fab flower.*

Plush palaces:
homes fit
for a
princess

When a princess isn't partying or performing her royal duties, she needs a place to lay her pretty head. Her perfect palace looks luxurious but feels homely. It's as lovely as she is – and just as warm and inviting.

Read on to find out how to turn your bedroom into a room fit for a princess.

Your dream palace

Think about your princess life. Will you need a window in a turret for Rapunzel moments? Or a glittering ballroom for the party of the century?

Use the amazing mansions on the right to inspire you as you sketch out a design for your own perfect palace.

don't forget a balcony for royal appearances

design a royal standard

decorate your palace with sparkling jewels

Pretty princess bedroom

Even if you don't live in a palace just yet, you can easily
add some royal razzle-dazzle to your princess pad.
It's easiest if you choose a theme – a color or style you
really love – to achieve a coordinated look.

jazz up your walls with *fun* frames

matching accessories add instant *glamor*

Treasure box

A princess needs somewhere to keep her jewels, her letters from Prince Charming, and her secret diary. Make your own special box.

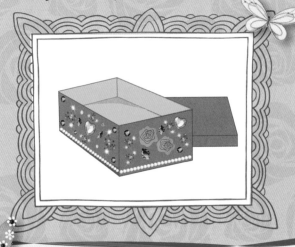

1 Mix equal amounts of bright paint and school glue and brush it over an old shoe box. Leave it to dry.

2 Decorate it with stickers, ribbons, buttons, stick-on jewels, colored foil, or tissue-paper flowers.

3 Be creative with your design by adding a crown or star to the decoration, outlined in glitter.

4 Using school glue, attach wrapping paper to the inside of the box to make a pretty lining.

use it to keep your diary and precious things safe!

Perfect photo frame

A heart-shaped frame shows how much you LOVE being a princess!

You will need:

- a pencil
- 2 pieces of card, the same size
- scissors*
- glue or sticky tape
- colored paper or stickers

An asterisk (*) means always ask an adult to help you with this step.

1 Draw a heart shape on one piece of card and cut it out carefully.*

2 Use glue or sticky tape to stick the two pieces of card together on three edges. Leave the top open.

3 Decorate the frame with colored paper or stickers. Slide a photo or drawing into the frame from the top.

make a hole in the top of the card and thread a pretty *ribbon* through the hole, then tie it in a bow to hang it up!

Bedroom bunting

1 Mark the midpoint on each edge of the card with a pencil.

2 Use a ruler to join the marks. Then cut out this diamond shape.*

3 Trace around the template on the back of the wrapping paper.

4 Cut out the diamond shapes and fold each one in half.*

5 Slip the shapes over the string and glue the sides together.

Bunting
adds instant glamor.
It's perfect for parties!

On your best
behavior: perfect
princess
poise

Are princesses too posh to be polite? No way!
A princess is always friendly and poised, putting
people she meets at ease. She treats others as she
would like to be treated – and everyone loves her
for it.

Here's how to have perfect princess poise,
whatever the occasion....

Princess Ps and Qs

A princess always minds her Ps and Qs, or "pleases" and "thank-yous," of course, but it's not just when she's speaking that Ps and Qs are part of her princess polish.

Banqueting behavior

It doesn't matter if she's dining at a banquet or enjoying tea for two. A real princess knows how to mind her manners.

she never talks with her *mouth full*

she listens *politely*, even if the chat is a bit dull!

she uses the correct *cutlery*, working from the outside in

A princess makes sure that everyone around her feels comfortable
– and that's really what good manners are all about.
She's never too grand to have a good time.

she chats to people on *either* side

she has *fun* and enjoys the party!

Being kind to others

A princess never forgets that she is privileged to live in a palace with everything her heart desires. She knows that helping others gives her even more pleasure than pleasing herself.

She is the first to volunteer when a charity needs helpers. She'll rattle a collection can, bake princess cakes for sale, or help with publicity.

Whether it's ailing animals or poorly people, a true princess is always ready to help others. She's quick to offer her princess possessions to charities when she doesn't need them and she cares about the environment, too.

a charity ball puts the *fun* in fundraising!

ROYAL CHARITY BALL

Curtsy like a princess

1 Bow your head to show respect, and hold the sides of your skirt.

2 Put your right foot a little behind your left foot, with your right heel off the ground.

3 Gracefully bend your knees, and slowly lower yourself down.

4 Just as gracefully, rise again to stand up straight.

a prince bows by nodding his head and bringing his shoulders forward slightly.

as you curtsy slowly and elegantly...

practice in a mirror and you will be the curtsy queen in no time!

Parties, princess-style

A perfect princess simply has to be the hostess with the mostest. She's charming, welcoming, and warm – and her parties are talked about for years afterwards.

Princess parties appear effortless, but a lot of work goes on behind the scenes. Luckily, as any savvy socialite knows, there are tips and tricks that will make any event amazing.

Invitations

Truly enticing invitations have two vital ingredients – info and allure. In other words, they tell your guests everything they need to know: the time, place, event, dress code, address for reply, and so on and they must be... well... inviting!

a decorative edging is princess pretty

HRH Princess Paula
invites you to a
Grand Imperial Ball

7:30 p.m. this Saturday
at the Pink Palace

RSVP: Pink Palace 12345

tell your guests what to bring

Please come to my
amaZZZing sleepover!

This Saturday at 7:00 p.m.
Bring a sleeping bag
and a teddy bear!

RSVP:
hrh@princessmail.com

Shhhhhh!
You've been invited
to a surprise party
for Princess Serena!

2:00 p.m. on Friday in
the Royal Park. Please
bring a balloon.

RSVP Princess Anna
555-123-1234

RSVP means *please reply!*

Buy pretty cards or make your own to match the theme of the party.

Have fun with your invitations. Use glitter to add sparkle, and play with shapes and colors. How about a royal scroll for a special party?

Preparty pamper

When her party is perfectly planned and prepared, a princess has time before her guests arrive to de-stress and make sure she's looking her radiant best.

You will need:

* a warm bath*
* cup of oatmeal (fine is best)
* pair of old tights or a knee-high
* scissors*

An asterisk (*) means always ask an adult to help you with this step.

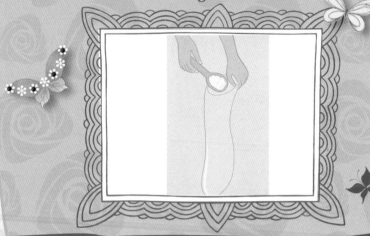

1 Cut the foot from a clean pair of old tights, about 8 inches (20 cm) long. Pour in the oatmeal and tie the top.*

2 Add the bag to a warm bath, squeezing it gently if you want.

3 Lie back and relax in a blissful bath for supersoft skin. Now you're ready… to get ready!

allow enough time to get ready without having to rush

Then put on your best smile and greet your guests!

Princess party

Every party is different. Don't be afraid to borrow ideas from events you've enjoyed. Remember: if your guests are happy and you're having fun, it's a perfect princess party!

confetti looks great on tables!

summer fruits look stylish!

welcome your guests with a *drink*

no party is complete without *music!*

It's fun to have a theme for the food and drink. Pink, perhaps?
Cranberry juice and ginger ale make the perfect princess punch,
while pink and purple cupcakes will tempt your guests!

Party games

Get the party started with some great music and giggly games.
They're perfect for breaking the ice and introducing people who
don't know each other.

For "The Name Game," put a simple
paper headband on each guest.
Each quest has to guess the name
on their band by asking others
questions, but answers can only be
"yes" or "no."

For "Sleeping Beauties," everyone
lies down and pretends to sleep. "The
Prince" makes jokes and comments.
The winner, who keeps still longest,
is crowned "Sleeping Beauty."

You've played "Pin the tail on the donkey," but how about "Stick the glass slipper on Cinderella"?

Super sleepovers

When you want to get together with your princess pals, there's nothing better than a palace sleepover.

Choose a theme you'll all enjoy, and don't forget that even princesses need their beauty sleep!

Choose a princess movie to watch – or even two!

make princess pink popcorn!

Give a prize for the most princessy pajamas!

Supply a few simple craft materials and make your own crazy crowns!

use fruit, ice cream, and sprinkles
to create Cinderella sundaes

make cupcakes and decorate them

Sleepover style

Why not host a style sleepover? Set up your bedroom as a beauty parlor, and invite your princess pals to give each other facials, manicures, massages, hairstyles, and make-up sessions. Look back at pages 24 to 55 for ideas.

don't forget relaxing **mood music**

take lots of *photos!*

pink towels and toiletries are perfect!

Mirror, mirror,
on the wall,
Who is the fairest
of them all?

Why, you are,
of course!

Travelling in style

When a princess leaves her palace for a party, she needs to travel in style, in something that suits her royal position and has room for a billowing ball gown.

In spring a glass coach is light and airy but keeps seasonal showers at bay.

An open carriage
is dreamy for
travelling to a
midsummer
night's ball.

Fall requires a
golden coach to suit the
season's hues.

In winter, a sumptuous
sleigh is the cosy way
to travel through
thick snow.

Design your perfect carriage

Design the carriage of your dreams, whether it is made of gold, glass, or ebony, large enough for your friends or just one perfect prince, and drawn by six gleaming black horses or a single white stallion, you can let your imagination go wild!

Don't forget to design the inside of your carriage, too. Will you sit on cream leather seats or relax on red velvet? Perhaps your carriage will have cushions to curl up with, decorated with bows, tassels, or buttons.

What type of handles will your carriage have? Clear crystal or glorious gold? Your feet will need a plush princess fabric to rest on, in a traditional coronet pattern, or something modern and stylish. The design decisions are yours!

The
perfect prince

Perhaps you've met him already, or simply seen him in your dreams. Whatever your perfect prince is like, one thing is certain: for him, you'll be the only princess in the world.

Prince predictor

Here's a fun way to find out what your perfect prince will be like and how you will meet him.

1 Fold a square of paper in half to make a triangle, then again to make a smaller triangle.

2 Open out the paper and fold each corner into the middle, making a square. Turn over and repeat.

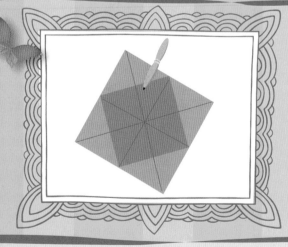

3 Unfold it and write your answers on the flaps, using the suggestions opposite, or make up your own!

4 Put your index finger and thumb of each hand in the flaps of the predictor to open and close it.

What to write on your predictor:

Front flaps – hair color: blond; brown; red; black

Inside flaps – personality: sporty; friendly; generous; thoughtful; romantic; caring; kind; brave

Under inside flaps – where you'll meet: at a ball; at a banquet; out horseback riding; on a yacht; at a wedding; at a garden party; at a concert; at a royal picnic

Your dream princess wedding

Every girl is a princess on her wedding day, but the marriage of a real princess is truly amazing. Every part of it has to be just perfect.

don't forget to design a cake and bouquet!

Whatever the bride wears her hair, it's *tiara time!*

her dress glitters with *sequins* or *crystals*

On her wedding day, a princess bride is radiant. Imagine what your wedding will be like!

Now draw your own wedding dress. Will it be a full, fairytale classic style or a sleek, modern design?

How to dance like Cinderella

1 Put your left hand on your prince's shoulder and your right in his hand at shoulder height.

2 Step back on your right foot, then back and to the left with your left, followed by your right foot.

3 Step forward with your left foot, then forward and right with your right, followed by your left foot.

4 Just keep repeating steps 2 and 3, following your prince's lead, as you slowly move around the dance floor.

your prince will guide you around the floor

Rate your princess progress

It's time to take the final test to see if you have what it takes to be a true princess!

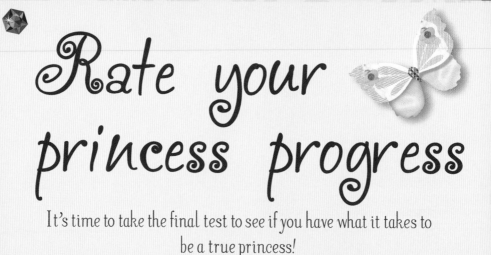

1. You long to see your princess pals. What do you invite them to?
a. A sleepover
b. A picnic
c. A grand ball

2. It's your wedding day! What is most important to you?
a. That all the people who have lined up to see you have a good view
b. That the sun shines all day long
c. That your dress and hair look perfect

3. You're having your hair done for a grand ball. What do you want?
a. Something you can forget about so you can concentrate on your friends
b. A style that will stay put, no matter how much you dance
c. An up-do to show off your tiara

4. Which word best describes you?
a. Loving
b. Lively
c. Stylish

5. What will your prince be like?
a. Friendly and warm
b. Sporty and energetic
c. Tall, dark, and handsome

6. At a party, a princess is wearing the same dress as you. What do you say?
a. Sorry, I'll change!
b. Let's do a dance routine!
c. You've got great taste!

Answers

Count your a, b, and c answers. Mostly a: Well done! You're a people person, a friend to everyone – a real princess. Mostly b: Congratulations! You have the energy and fun factor of a true princess. Mostly c: Excellent! Beautiful and poised, you're everyone's idea of a real princess. A mixture of a, b, and c: Sensational! You've got it all, your royal highness!

Your top-to-toe princess checklist

Before you step out of your palace, make a quick check that you are princess perfect.

your hair is *shiny* and *styled*

you are poised and *smiling!*

your skin is *clear* and *glowing*

your jewelry *sparkles!*

your feet and hands are *lovely!*

your dress has princess *pizzazz.*

Now that you know all there is to being a princess, it's time to live...

happily ever after!

Princess words

Balcony
A small platform outside a building, reached from a window

Carriage
A four-wheeled vehicle pulled by two or more horses

Charm (1)
A small metal decoration or jewel

Charm (2)
Attractiveness

Chic
Stylish and elegant

Chiffon
Very light, sheer fabric

Clutch bag
A small bag with no strap

Coach
A state carriage, used for important occasions

Confetti
Tiny pieces of colored paper or petals thrown at celebrations

Conveyance
A vehicle

Dolly bag
A bag with a drawstring to close it

Ebony
A kind of wood, nearly black in color

Fabric
Woven, knitted, or felted material

Fairytale
A magical story with a happy ending

Fan
Paper stretched over a frame that you wave to make a cooling breeze

Floral
Covered or filled with flowers

Fringe
A border of hanging threads

Gem
A precious stone, cut to make it shine

Glamor
Magical beauty

Jewel
An ornament with precious stones

Luxurious
Expensive and enjoyable

Mansion
A grand house

Motif
A small design idea

Palace
A grand home for important people, such as princesses

Pastel
A light color

Poise
Calm, controlled, thoughtful behavior

Pom-pom
A round ornament made of tightly bunched ribbons, threads, or flowers

Princess
A royal girl or woman, often the daughter of a king, queen, prince, or princess

Privileged
Having special advantages

Pump
A light, flat shoe for dancing or sports

Radiant
Dazzling or glowing

Season
Time of year: winter, spring, summer, or fall

Sequin
A tiny, shiny decoration

Shawl
A large piece of material, usually worn draped over the shoulders or head

Sheer
Almost see-through or transparent

Shoulder bag
A bag with a long strap

Sleigh
A vehicle with runners instead of wheels for travelling over snow, pulled by horses, dogs, or reindeer

Standard
A flag

Tassel
An ornament made of a bunch of hanging threads

Tiara
A small, light crown or band, usually very sparkly

Train
A long piece of material stretching from the back of a dress, which may drag along the ground or be carried by servants

Turret
A small tower in a castle or palace

Volunteer
Someone who offers to work without payment

Index

B
Bags 22–23
Balls 91
Banquets 88–89
Beauty secrets 24–37, 106–107
Bedrooms 76-77, 82–83
Behavior 84–93
Birthstones 58–59
Boots 20
Bowing 93
Bunting 76, 82–83
Butterfly motifs 13
C
Charity work 90-91
Charms 22
Cinderella 103, 118
Cloaks 18
Colors 12, 14, 16, 17, 18, 22, 101, 106
Craft ideas 62–71, 78–83, 104, 114–115
Crystals 22, 111, 117
Cupcakes 90, 101, 105
Curtsying 92–93
Cutlery 88
D
Dancing 21, 91, 118–119
Diaries 78–79
Drinks 101
E
Environment 90

Exercise 25
Eyes 28
F
Fabrics 11, 12, 14, 15, 18, 111
Facials 26–29
Fall 17–17, 46–47, 109
Fans 14
Fashion 10–23
Feathers 22
Feet 15, 20–21, 36–37, 122
Flags 75
Flowers 12, 13, 22, 50, 53, 54, 70–71, 116
Food 25, 88–89, 100–101, 104, 105, 116
Friendship 68–69, 87, 104–105
Frills 12
Fringes 22
Fruit 100, 105
G
Gems 11, 12, 14, 16, 19, 21, 22, 49, 56–67, 71, 75, 78–79
H
Hairstyles 15, 17, 38–55, 122
Hair treatments 40–41
Hand care 30, 122
Healthy eating 25
Heart motifs 13, 80–81
I
Ice cream 105
Invitations 87, 96–97

J

Jewelry 11, 12, 14, 16, 17, 18, 19, 21, 22, 49,
    56–71, 77, 78–79, 122

K

Keeping cool 14–15

Keeping warm 16, 18

Kindness 6, 90–91

M

Manners 6, 84–93

Marriage 116–117

Massage 26, 30, 36, 106

Mirrors 93, 107

Motifs 13

Movies 104

Music 101, 102, 106

N

Nail polish 30–37, 107

Nails 30–37,

P

Pajamas 104

Palaces 72–75

Pampering 24–37, 98–99, 106–107

Parties 87, 94–111

Party games 102–103

Photo frames 80–81

Photos 106

Politeness 84–93

Pom-poms 20

Presents 87

Princes 112–119

Pumps 20

Q

Quizzes 8–9, 120–121

S

Sandals 15, 21

Scarves 15

Seasonal style 11–21

Sequins 22, 117

Shawls 16

Shoes 15, 20–21, 37

Sleep 25, 104

Sleepovers 104–107

Spring 12–13, 42–43, 108

Standards 75

Star motifs 13

Summer 14–15, 21, 44–45, 109

Sun care 15, 29

Sunglasses 15, 29

Sunlight 14

T

Tassels 22, 111

Tiaras 12, 18, 55, 60–61, 117

Toenails 36–37

Travel 108–111

Treasure box 78–79

W

Weather 16, 18

Weddings 116–117

Winter 18–19, 48–49, 109

Wraps 16

An Hachette UK Company
www.hachette.co.uk

First published in the USA in 2014 by Ticktock, an imprint of Octopus Publishing Group Ltd
Endeavour House, 189 Shaftesbury Avenue, London WC2H 8JY
www.octopusbooks.co.uk
www.octopusbooksusa.com
www.ticktockbooks.com

Distributed in the US by Hachette Book Group USA
237 Park Avenue, New York N Y 10017, USA

Distributed in Canada by Canadian Manda Group
165 Dufferin Street, Toronto, Ontario, Canada M6K 3H6

ISBN 978 178325 085 1

Printed and bound in China

1 3 5 7 9 10 8 6 4 2

Author: Nicola Baxter Artists: Anita Romeo and Diane Kolar
Series Editor: Sue McMillan Design: Alison Gadsby
Publisher: Tim Cook Managing Editor: Karen Rigden Production: Lucy Carter

Photography: Gavin Sawyer for Roddy Paine Studios